NAVIES OF THE SECOND WORLD WAR

JAPANESE BATTLESHIPS AND CRUISERS

MACDONALD : LONDON

First published in the Japanese language by
Shuppan Kyodo-sha, Tokyo
First published in the English language in 1963 by
Macdonald & Co. (Publishers) Ltd.,
St. Giles House, 49/50 Poland Street, London, W. 1
Second Edition 1968
Made and printed in Japan

SBN 356 01475 4

FOREWORD

Incredibly rapid expansion had made Japan a major maritime power, but the destruction which followed her defeat had been equally swift and complete. With the end of the war Japan was thrown into confusion. A navy which had once been the pride of the nation was forgotten as were all other things military. But, by the end of a decade the new Japan was a stable reality. It was in this context that people began to ask questions about the war and the Services. Particular public interest was directed at the navy, its war strategies and resources.

This interest was natural enough since the war in the Pacific was essentially a series of naval battles and operations. An analysis by experts in terms of the naval strategies and tactics involved would provide one sort of answer, but so long as there was no account which made available informed and detailed particulars of the individual ships concerned, it would have been difficult to reach any balanced assessment on the actions of the Imperial Japanese Navy.

It was with this thought in mind that our book was compiled, and with the kind co-operation of Macdonald & Co. (Publishers) Ltd., London, has been made available to readers all over the world. While this book deals with battleships and cruisers, a second sister volume is devoted to aircraft carriers and destroyers. In essence pictorial, the two books contain full particulars of individual ships as well as their history in action up to the end of the Pacific War.

It is our hope that readers will find in these books and in subsequent books in the series about the other Services a valuable guide to the understanding of Japan's war.

The Publishers.

INDEX

Foreword

BATTLESHIPS

CRUISERS

BATTLESHIPS

KONGO Class

	Completed	Converted	Fate
KONGO	16-8-13	1) 31- 3-31	Lost 21-11-44, Battle for Leyte
	Vickers	2) 8- 1-37	Gulf, U.S. submarine
HIEI	4-8-14	1) 31-12-32	Lost 13-11-42 Battle of Guadalcanal, U.S.
	Yokosuka	2) 31- 1-40	planes
HARUNA	19-4-15	1) 31- 7-28	Scrapped after war
	Kawasaki	2) 30- 9-34	
KIRISHIMA	19-4-15	1) 31- 3-30	Lost 15-11-42, Battle of Guadalcanal, U.S.
	Nagasaki	2) 8- 6-36	ships

Project : 1910 Expansion Programme and 1911 Emergency Expansion Programme.

History : The mightiest battle-cruiser at completion, the *KONGO* was built in England followed by her sister ships built in Japan making use of British technology. Through extensive conversion and modernisation conducted from late 1920s these battle-cruisers were given stronger protection to become battleships, there speed being reduced from 27.5 kts. to 25.9 kts. Named after famous mountains in Japan for their original category of the battle-cruiser, they emerged from the second conversion programme of late 1930s as unique modern high-speed battleships with a maximum speed of 30 kts. The *HIEI* was converted into a training battleship in 1932 as a result of the London Naval Treaty but joined her sister-ships later on, after being rebuilt as a high-speed battleship as soon as the non-treaty days arrived.

(Right) : The battle-cruiser *KONGO* off Shinagawa, April 1922, the flag at half-mast for the state funeral of Field Marshal A. Yamagata.

BCR KONGO.

The four high-speed battleships of the *Kongo* Class comprised the Third Battleship Division and operated with the carrier task forces in the Pacific War. The *HIEI* became the first battleship Japan lost in the war when she was scuttled after receiving heavy damage from U.S. torpedo-bombers off Savo Island.

Comparable Ships: *Repulse* (Br.),

1) Displacement: 26,330 T. (WS), 27,963 t. (WN)
   Dimensions: Length: 704.03 ft.-214.58 m (o.a.), 695.00 ft.-211.84 m. (w.l.)
   Beam: 92.00 ft-28.04 m. (w.l.)   Draught: 27.50 ft.-8.38 m. (mean)
   Armament: Guns: 8-14 in. 16-5.9 in.,   Torpedo Tubes: 8-21 in. (under waterline)
   Machinery: Parsons Turbines   S.H.P.: 64,000   Speed: 27.5 kts.
   Complement: 1,221

2) Displacement: 31,720 T. (WS), 36,314 t. (WT)
   Dimensions: Length: 728.55 ft.-222.05 m (o.a.), 720.54 ft.-218.61 m. (w.l.)
   Beam: 95.28 ft.-29.04 m. (w.l.)   Draught: 31.98 ft.-9.72 m. (mean)
   Armament: Guns: 8-14 in., 14-5.9 in., 8-5 in. AA. 20-25 mm. AA.
   Planes: 3   Catapult: 1
   Machinery: Kanpon Turbines   S.H.P.: 136,000   Speed: 30.27 kts.
   Complement: 1,437
   Data: 1) At completion (HARUNA)., 2) After second conversion (KONGO).

KONGO (2)

(Right)   The battle-cruiser *KONGO* in mid-1925s. Addition of the direction control post in the foremast, extension of the No.1 funnel with the new smokehood, addition of the searchlight tower between the Nos. 2 and 3 funnels, etc. considerably changed the silhouette of the ship since the time of completion. Armament of the ship comprised eight 45-cal. 36-cm. (14-in.) main guns, sixteen 15-cm. (5.9-in.) guns and eight 8-cm. (3.2-in.) guns.

BCR KONGO.

KONGO (3)

The battleship *KONGO* dressed for the 1933 Naval Review. The aircraft carrier *AKAGI* is seen in the right background. The *KONGO* shown in this picture is after the first conversion that turned her from a battle-cruiser to a battleship. The conversion, made within limitations of the Washington Naval Treaty, was mainly aimed at modernization of the fire control system and increased armour protection. With less than 3,000 tons increase in the standard displacement, the bulge was also added to the sides. The machinery, however, remained same and her speed after the first conversion was reduced to 25.9 knots.

BB KONGO.

KONGO (4)

The battleship *KONGO* making 24 knots off the Bay of Tokyo in the Spring of 1942 on her way to Yokosuka from the South Pacific theatre. The white colours on the top of the pagoda mast denotes that the ship is under the direct command of the Commander-in-Chief, Combined Fleet.

Note the Rising Sun flags spread on B and X turrets for aerial identification. The second conversion of the *Kongo* Class was primarily to achieve higher speed: the machinery was changed and the stern was extended by 24 feet.

BB KONGO.

HIEI (1)

The battle-cruiser *HIEI* shortly after completion. Construction of the *HIEI* began ten months after the work was initiated on her sister ship *KONGO* in Britain. The *HIEI* used both coal-fired and oil-fired boilers, carrying 1,000 tons of oil and 4,000 tons of coal.

BCR HIEI.

HIEI (2)

The battle-cruiser *HIEI* in 1929. Addition of the fire control system and the direction finder, etc. in the foremast had changed her appearance since completion. Distance between the Nos. 1 and 2 funnels is shorter on the *HIEI* and two other ships of this class built in Japan than on the *KONGO* which was built in England. The angular shaped main turret sides were peculier to *HIEI* and *KONGO* only.

BCR HIEI.

HIEI (3)

(Right): The *HIEI* as training battleship in 1933. The military authoritaties obliterated with white the background of the pictures of warships taken for commercial sales (such as this one) to keep secret the places where the pictures were taken. Under the restrictions of the London Naval Treaty, the No.4 main gun turret and all of the secondary guns were dismantled; the number of boilers was reduced and the side armour plates were removed in the course of conversion ended on 31st December 1932. The fore funnel became thinner.

Training BB HIEI.

The high-speed battleship *HIEI* on full speed official trial run on 5th December 1939, off Sukumo Bay, Shikoku Island. Conversion of the *HIEI* from the training battleship was started in November 1936, incorporating various new designs and technology. Her pagoda mast structure especially served as the prototype for that of the *YAMATO*. The complicated pagoda mast structure includes (from top to bottom) the main gun fire control post, the 10-m. (32.8-ft.) dual range finder, the anti-aircraft combat centre, the combat bridge, the searchlight control post, the compass bridge, the 4.5-m. (14.8-ft.) range finder and the control cabin (immediately aft and above the No.2 main turret).

BB HIEI.

HARUNA   (1)

The battle-cruiser *HARUNA* shortly after completion in **1915.**
The third ship of the *Kongo* Class, the *HARUNA* was completed
on 19th April 1915 after a total 37 months work and at a cost
of ¥24.5 million.   Initially the *HARUNA* was equipped with
eight 53-cm. (21-in.) underwater torpedo tubes.   The simple
tripod foremast was soon to be modified to accomodate the fire
control post and other command centres to become the so-called
pagoda mast.

BCR HARUNA.

23

HARUNA (2)

The battleship *HARUNA* in 1930, after the first conversion.
The No. 1 funnel of the *HARUNA* in those days was a little
thicker than that of the *KIRISHIMA*. Between the Nos. 3 and
4 turrets can be seen a Type 90 Model 3 floatplane and the
derrick.

BB HARUNA

HARUNA (3)   The high-speed battleship *HARUNA* at Tokyo Bay in October 1935. She attained a maximum speed of 30.2 kts. on the official full speed trial run. Through the second conversion, the main gun fire control systems, the living quarters, the damage control system, etc. were all modernised. Emergency flooding and pumping systems were also effected immediately before the Pacific War. The height of the No. 2 funnel was later made equal to the No. 1 funnel.

BB HARUNA.

KIRISHIMA (1)

The battle-cruiser *KIRISHIMA* on her way from Nagasaki to Sasebo in April 1915, following completion at the Nagasaki shipyard of the Mitsubishi Shipbuilding Co. on 19th April. Armour plating of the *KIRISHIMA* was 7 inches on sides and 10 inches on the control tower, respectively thinner by two inches than that of the battleship *FUSO*.

BCR KIRISHIMA.

KIRISHIMA (2)

The battleship *KIRISHIMA* after the first conversion. She is seen at Yokosuka in 1932 as the second ship of the First Battleship Division. The ship is equipped with a derrick but no catapult as yet.

BB KIRISHIMA.

KIRISHIMA (3)

The battleship *KIRISHIMA* at Sukumo Bay, off Shikoku Island, in May 1937.

Note the huge platform for 25-mm. anti-aircraft guns in front of the pagoda mast, and the lengthened stern. On the catapult is seen one of the three Type 95 float reconnaissance biplanes.

The second conversion of the *Kongo* Class ships was conducted first with the *HARUNA* and then *KONGO* and *KIRISHIMA*, and finally with the *HIEI*. Thus, there were slight differences among these ships: in the standard displacement the *HARUNA* was 32,156 tons, the *KONGO* 31,720 tons, the *KIRISHIMA* 31,980 tons, and the *HIEI* 32,350 tons. The two secondary guns located nearest to the bow were removed during 1937.

BB KIRISHIMA.

FUSO Class

Name	Completed	Converted	Fate
FUSO	8–11–15	1) 12–5–33	Lost 25–10–44, Battle for Leyte Gulf, U.S. ships.
	Kure	2) 19–2–35	
YAMASHIRO	31–3–17	30–3–35	Lost 25–10–44, Battle for Leyte Gulf, U.S. ships.
	Yokosuka		

Project: 1911–12 Emergency Expansion Programme

History: Japan's first super-dreadnought battleships, the *Fuso* Class ships were built to form the main force which would operate in concert with the four battle-cruisers of the *Kongo* Class. Named after the provinces of the Old Japan for the category of the battleship, the *FUSO* and *YAMASHIRO* underwent extensive conversion from 1933 through 1935 in the first phase of the battleship modernisation programme. The *FUSO*, being the first ship to be converted, lacked refinement in the silhouette and was generally regarded as the ugliest battleship of the Imperial Japanese Navy. The *YAMASHIRO* had a far better appearance.

Old and slow, the two battleships were assigned to second-lined duties during the Pacific War. When the Imperial Japanese Navy threw in everything it had in the Battle for Leyte Gulf, the *FUSO* and *YAMASHIRO* formed the Second Battleship Division and made their way into the strait of Surigao only to find their graves there after putting up a valiant fight.

Comparable Ships: *Royal Sovereign* (Br.), *Nevada* (U.S.), *Pennsylvania* (U.S.), *Bretagne* (Fr.), *Marat* (Sov. Union)

(Right): The battleship *FUSO* on official trial run on 29th August 1915, making 23 kts. with a displacement of 30,662 tons.

BB FUSO.

1) **Displacement:** 29,330 T. (WS), 31,785 t. (WN)
   Dimensions: Length: 653.03 ft.-205.13 m (o.a.), 665.00 ft.-202.69 m. (w.l.)
   Beam: 94.00 ft.-28.65 m. (w.l.)   Draught: 28.50 ft.-8.62 m. (mean)
   Armament: Guns: 12-14 in., 16-5.9 in., 4-1 in. AA.   Torpedo Tubes: 6-21 in. (under waterline)
   Machinery: Curtis Turbines   S.H.P.: 40,000   Speed: 23.0 kts.
   Complement: 1,193

2) **Displacement:** 34,700 T. (WS), 39,154 t. (WT)
   Dimensions: Length: 698.03 ft.-212.75 m. (o.a.), 689.01 ft.-210.00 m. (w.l.)
   Beam: 100.53 ft.-30.64 m. (w.l.)   Draught: 31.79 ft.-9.69 m. (mean)
   Armament: Guns: 12-14 in., 14-5.9 in., 8-5 in. AA., 20-25 mm. AA.   Planes: 3   Catapult: 1
   Machinery: Kanpon Turbines   S.H.P.: 76,889   Speed: 24.7 kts.
   Complement: 1,296
   Data: (FUSO) 1) At completion., 2) After conversion.

FUSO (2)

(Right): The battleship *FUSO* in 1924, with the cruiser *CHIKUMA*,
the flagship of the first Submarine Squadron, in the right background. Completed in 1915 together with battleships *HARUNA*
and *KIRISHIMA*, the *FUSO* came to possess the so-called pagoda
mast where various command centres were concentrated. Anti-
torpedo net device on the sides was removed from all battleships by 1926.

BB FUSO.

BB FUSO.

FUSO (3)

The battleship *FUSO* on manoeuvres immediately before the Pacific War.

(Right): The battleship *FUSO* at Tokyo Bay in October 1935. In those days there were long debates concerning the advantages and disadvantages of mounting the main armament in six twin turrets as on the *Fuso* Class or four triple turrets of the U. S. *Pensylvania* Class. The Japanese was considered better for attacking while the U. S. arrangement was thought superior from the defensive point of view.

FUSO (4)

BB FUSO.

YAMASHIRO (1)

The battleship *YAMASHIRO* at Yokosuka in April 1917. With completion of the *YAMASHIRO*, Japan came to possess a super-dreadnought which was 10,000 tons heavier than the *SETTSU*.

BB YAMASHIRO.   *41*

YAMASHIRO (2)

The *YAMASHIRO* at Yokosuka in 1928. Note the modified pagoda mast, the searchlight tower in front of the No.2 funnel, etc. The anti-torpedo net device on the sides had been removed by this time.

BB YAMASHIRO.

YAMASHIRO (3)

The battleship *YAMASHIRO* after conversion. Through experience gained with her sister ship *FUSO*, the catapult of the *YAMASHIRO* was installed at stern instead of the top of the No.3 turret. Pictured in October 1935, the *YAMASHIRO* was then the flagship of the Combined Fleet.

BB YAMASHIRO.

ISE Class

Name	Completed	Converted	Fate
ISE	15-12-17	1) 23- 3-37	Scrapped after war
	Nagasaki	2) 5- 9-43	
HYUGA	30- 4-18	1) 7- 9-36	Scrapped after war
	Kawasaki	2) 30-11-43	

Project : 1912 Emergency Expansion Programme.

History : Improvement of the *Fuso* Class, the *Ise* Class ships differed in arrangement of the Nos. 3 and 4 main turrets. After conversion of 1936–37, they somewhat resembled the *Idaho* Class ships of the U. S. Navy. After the outbreak of the Pacific War, the Nos. 5 and 6 main turrets were removed for installation of a flight deck, to make the two battleships into unprecedented carrier-battleships. They, however, had no opportunity to prove the merits of this new concept as the war turned against Japan. In the Battle for Leyte Gulf, they comprised part of the last Japanese task force. Despite heavy damage both survived the battle and returned to Kure, where they remained inoperative until the end of war due to damage by U. S. air raids.

Comparable Ships : *Royal Sovereign* (Br.), *Idaho* (U. S.), *California* (U. S.)

(Right) : The battleship *ISE* at Yokohama in April 1922 to welcome the Prince of Wales.

1) **Displacement:** 29,990 T. (WS), 32,063 t. (WN)
   Dimensions: *Length:* 683.03 ft.-208.18 m. (o.a.), 673.00 ft.-205.74 m. (w.l.)
   Beam: 94.00 ft.-28.65 m. (w.l.) *Draught:* 27.08 ft.-8.86 m. (mean)
   Armament: *Guns:* 12-14 in., 20-5.5 in., 4-1 in. AA. *Torpedo Tubes:* 6-21 in. (under waterline)
   Machinery: Curtis Turbines *S.H.P.:* 45,000 *Speed:* 23.6 kts.
   Complement: 1,360

2) **Displacement:** 35,800 T. (WS), 40,169 t. (WT)
   Dimensions: *Length:* 708.04 ft.-215.80 m. (o.a.), 700.03 ft.-213.36 m. (w.l.)
   Beam: 104.12 ft.-31.75 m. (w.l.) *Draught:* 31.00 ft.-9.45 m. (mean)
   Armament: *Guns:* 12-14 in., 16-5.5 in., 8-5 in. AA., 20-25 mm. AA. *Planes:* 3 *Catapult:* 1
   Machinery: Kanpon Turbines *S.H.P.:* 80,000 *Speed:* 25.25 kts.
   Complement: 1,376

3) **Displacement:** 35,350 T. (WS), 38,676 t. (WT)
   Dimensions: *Length:* 721.82 ft.-219.62 m. (o.a.), 700.03 ft.-213.36 m. (w.l.)
   Beam: 104.12 ft.-31.75 m. (w.l.) *Draught:* 29.61 ft.-9.03 m. (mean)
   Armament: *Guns:* 8-14 in., 16-5 in. AA., 108-25 mm. AA., 180-4.7 in. rockets (after aircraft had been removed and extra AA. guns sited on the flight deck)
   Planes: 22 *Catapults:* 2 (removed after the Battle for Leyte Gulf)
   Machinery: Kanpon Turbines *S.H.P.:* 80,000 *Speed:* 25.0 kts.
   Complement: 1,463
   Data: 1) At completion., 2) After conversion., 3) After conversion to battleship/carrier.

(Right): The battleship *ISE* in September 1931. Note the unique pagoda mast which accommodates the main gun direction finder at top. Searchlight platform was installed around the No.2 funnel and the main mast was extended.

BB ISE.

ISE (3)

The battleship *ISE* during Naval exercises in the Pacific in July 1938.

Twelve main guns and the range finder are directed to port, ready for firing six-gun salvoes alternately. The Imperial Japanese Navy possessed a total 80 45-cal 14-inch main guns fitted on eight battleships.

On the stern are seen two type 95 floatplanes on catapult. Identification of the *ISE* from her sister ship *HYUGA* may be based on the different relative locations of the main mast and the aft bridge. The *ISE*, after conversion, had ten 25-mm. machine guns and their AA. fire control system.

BB ISE.

ISE (4)

The carrier-battleship *ISE* on her official full speed trial run on
24th August 1943.   Defeat at Midway forced the Japanese Navy
to map out an emergency carrier construction programme under
which a total of four battleships of the *Ise* and *Fuso* classes
were to become carrier-battleships.   But only two ships of
the *Ise* Class were rebuilt, those of the *Fuso* Class being with-
drawn from the programme after the Battle of the Marianas.
Armament of the carrier-battleship *ISE* comprised eight 36-cm.
main guns, no secondary guns, sixteen 12.7-cm. (5-in.) anti-aircraft
guns and six 12-cm. (4.7-in.) rocket guns (6×30). She was originally
scheduled to carry twenty-two 13-shi experimental dive bombers
(Judy) but this was later changed **to** 14-shi floatplane dive
bombers (Paul).

Carrier-Battleship ISE. 53

HYUGA (1)

The battleship *HYUGA* shortly after completion in late April 1918 at the Kawasaki Shipyard. For efficient fire control and protection, the six main gun turrets are grouped into three sets, a distinction from the *Fuso* Class ships.

BB HYUGA.

HYUGA (2)

(Right): The battleship *HYUGA* in 1932. The pagoda mast was completed between 1930-31 as was the case with the *ISE*. At that time the ship was not yet equipped with a catapult although a derrick was installed for floatplanes. The ship's living quarters were notoriously uncomfortable.

BB HYUGA.

HYUGA (3)

The battleship *HYUGA* on the eve of the war in 1941. The ship was used as a target ship for practice torpedo attacks by Type 1 (Betty) land-based bombers. The *HYUGA* was also used to evolve tactics against aerial torpedoes.

After conversion in 1936, the *HYUGA* was equipped with mixed anti-aircraft armament of 40-mm. and 13-mm. (0.5-in.) guns in twin mountings. In 1940, however, these guns were replaced by ten 25-mm. twin guns.

BB HYUGA.

HYUGA (4)

The carrier-battleship *HYUGA* as seen in November 1943. Nos. 5 and 6 main gun turrets and all of the secondary gun casemates were removed. The flight deck, a large hangar and two catapults were installed astern. Anti-aircraft armament was augmented to sixteen 12.7-cm. (5-in.) guns and nineteen triple mountings of 25-mm. guns. Atop the pagoda mast is a Type 2 Model 1 radar.

Carrier-Battleship HYUGA.

NAGATO Class

Name	Completed	Converted	Fate
NAGATO	25–11–20	1) 1924	Lost 29–11–46, Bikini Atoll, U.S. A-bomb test
	Kure	2) 31–1–36	
MUTSU	24–10–21	1) 1924	Lost 8–6–43, Inland Sea, accidental explosion.
	Yokosuka	2) 30–9–36	

Project: New Ship Building Programme of 1916.

History: The names of these two battleships will be long remembered as the representative battleships of the Imperial Japanese Navy and also the world's first capital ships to carry 40-cm. (16-in.) guns. Originally a two stacker, a funnel cap was installed on the No. 1 funnel in 1921. The middle part of the No. 1 funnel was bent rearwards in 1924. Through conversion in 1936, the two funnels were replaced with a newly-designed single funnel.

During the Pacific War, the two battleships comprised the First Battleship Division, the *NAGATO* being the flagship of the Combined Fleet, until the appearance of the *YAMATO* and *MUSASHI*.

The *MUTSU* at anchor off Hashirajima in the Inland Sea was sunk by an explosion, the cause of which remains a mystery even today. The *NAGATO* survived the war and was used as one the "guinea pigs" to determine the effect of the A-bomb blast conducted by the U.S. at the Bikini Atoll.

Comparable Ships: *Nelson* (Br.), *Maryland* (U.S.)

BBs MUTSU & NAGATO.

1)	Displacement:	32,720 T. (WS), 34,116 t. (WN),		
	Dimensions:	*Length:* 708.04 ft.-215.80 m. (o.a.),	*Beam:* 95.00 ft.-28.96 m. (w.l.)	
		Draught: 30.01 ft.- 9.08 m. (mean)		
	Armament:	*Guns:* 8-16 in., 20-5.5 in., 4-1 in. AA. *Torpedo Tubes:* 8-21 in.		
	Machinery:	Gihon Turbines *S.H.P.:* 80,000 *Speed:* 26.5 kts.		
	Complement:	1,333		
2)	Displacement:	39,130 T. (WS), 43,581 t. (WT), 46,356 t. (WF)		
	Dimensions:	*Length:* 734.03 ft.-224.94 m. (o.a.), 725.33 ft.-221.07 m. (w.l.)		
		Beam: 108.13 ft.-32.96 m. (w.l.) *Draught:* 31.13 ft.-9.49 m. (mean)		
	Armament:	*Guns:* 8-16 in., 18-5.5 in., 8-5 in. AA., 20-25 mm. AA.		
		Planes: 3 *Catapult:* 1		
	Machinery:	Kanpon Turbines *S.H.P.:* 82.300 *Speed:* 25.0 kts.		
	Complement:	1,368		
	Data:	1) (NAGATO) At completion., 2) After conversion.		

NAGATO (2)

(Right): The battleship *NAGATO* in late 1920s. The pagoda mast and
the unique No.1 funnel gave a distinct silhouette to the *Nagato*
Class ships. They were the world's first capital ships to carry
eight 40-cm. main guns.

BB NAGATO.

NAGATO (3)

The battleship *NAGATO* on the eve of the Pacific War in 1941.

The black stripes at the front of the main gun turrets are 250-mm. armour plating added during the conversion.

BB NAGATO.

NAGATO (4)

(Right): The *NAGATO* at anchor off Brunei on 22nd October **1944**, prior to the Battle for Leyte Gulf. Atop the pagoda mast is a Type 2 Model 1 radar (No. 21 rader) and on the side of the main mast is a Type 1 Model 3 (No. 13) radar. A Type 0 (F1M2) spotter biplane is seen at stern.

BB NAGATO.

BB NAGATO.

NAGATO (5)

The *NAGATO* as seen from a British warship at Amoy in 1938. Through conversion of 1936, displacement was increased by 6,000 tons. The single funnel with the searchlight platform, the reinforced pagoda mast, the derrick, and the long side bulge, etc, gave a new silhouette to the old battleship.

BB MUTSU.

MUTSU (1) The battleship *MUTSU* on her official trial run on 24th October 1921, with, 33,800-ton displacement. Armament comprised eight 40-cm. 45-cal. guns in four twin turrets and her maximum speed was 26.5 kts.

MUTSU (2)

The *MUTSU* in 1923. The funnel cap was fitted on the No. 1 funnel and searchlights installed on both masts.

BB MUTSU.   *71*

MUTSU (3)

(Left): The *MUTSU* in the Inland Sea in 1924. It was in this year that the No.1 funnel was bent rearward.

BB MUTSU.

BB MUTSU.

MUTSU (4)

The *MUTSU* in 1940, at full speed in heavy weather.
Displacement and speed of the *MUTSU*, after conversion, were
39,050 tons standard and 25.3 knots respectively.

BB MUTSU.

The *MUTSU* as seen from a British warship at Amoy in 1938.
The main guns could be trained at the maximum elevation of 43
degrees and had a range of 37,000 metres (23 miles).
Firing rate was one salvo every 40 seconds. The derrick on the
MUTSU is positioned a little different from that of the *NAGATO*.

YAMATO Class

Name:	Completed	Fate
YAMATO	16–12–41 Kure	Lost 7–4–45, Battle off Bonomisaki, U.S. planes
MUSASHI	5– 8–42 Nagasaki	Lost 24–10–44, Battle for Leyte Gulf, U.S. planes
SHINANC	19–11–44 Yokosuka (as carrier)	Lost 29–11–44 off Shionomisaki, U.S. submarine
No. 111.		Construction began on 7–11–40 but work was suspended and the ship scrapped.

Project : 3rd Reinforcement Programme of 1937 (*YAMATO* and *MUSASHI*), 4th Reinforcement programme of 1939 (*SHINANO* and *No.111*)

History : The *Yamato* Class battleships were the last, and the largest ships of the long battleship era. Their existance was a top secret.

When the war ended and everything about them became known, they were no longer in existence. Thus, they are like the "Phantom Giants" to the average Japanese.

The *Yamato* Class was conceived as the trump card of the Japanese Navy to cope with quantity in the heated race of warship construction among the world's major powers. A unique product of a "have-not", it was intended to outrange enemy's 40-cm. gun battleships with the 46-cm. (18-in) guns. The Battleship Era, however, was being superseded by the Era of the Aeroplane even when their construction began. The *YAMATO* and *MUSASHI* were both sunk by aerial attacks.

(Right): The battleship *YAMATO* making 27 knots on her official trial run in 1941.

76

BB YAMATO.

The *SHINANO*, after the Battle of Midway, was converted into the world's biggest carrier. It was ironical then that she was sunk by a U.S. submarine only ten days after her completion and on her first operational cruise.

No.111, the fourth ship of the *Yamato* Class, was not completed due to the outbreak of the Pacific War.

Comparable Ships: *Vanguard* (Br.), *Iowa* (U.S.), *Bismarck* (Gr.)

Displacement :	65,000 T. (WS), 69,100 t. (WT), 72,809 t. (WF)
Dimensions :	*Length :* 862.90 ft.-263.00 m. (o.a.), 839.94 ft.-256.00 m. (w.l.)
	Beam : 121.07 ft.-36.90 m. (w.l.) *Draught :* 35.58 ft.-10.86 m. (mean)
Armament :	*Guns :* 9–18 in., 12–6.1 in., 12–5 in. AA., 24–25 mm. AA., 4–12.7 mm. AA.
	YAMATO-24-5 in. AA., 147-25 mm. AA., 4-13 mm. AA. (April 1945) MUSASHI-12-5 in.
	AA., 130-25 mm. AA., 4-13 mm. AA. (Oct. 1944)
	Planes : 7 *Catapults :* 2
Machinery :	Kanpon Turbines *S.H.P. :* 150,000 *Speed :* 27.46 kts.
Complement :	2,500
Data :	At completion. (YAMATO)

(Right): The battleship *MUSASHI* at Bruney in October 1944.

BB MUSASHI

HEAVY CRUISERS

FURUTAKA Class

Name	Completed	Converted	Fate
FURUTAKA	31-3-26 Nagasaki	30- 4-36	Lost 12-10-42, Battle off Cape Esperance, U.S. cruisers and destroyers
KAKO	20-7-26 Kawasaki	27-12-37	Lost 9-8-42, entrance of Port Gabieng, U.S. submarine

Project: New Reinforcement Programme under Washington Naval Treaty in 1923.

History: The *FURUTAKA* and *KAKO* were the first two ships to carry 20-cm. (7.9-in.) main guns, an armament which made them belong to the category of the heavy cruiser. Designed by the world famous naval architect, Vice Admiral Dr. Yuzuru Hiraga, they surprised the world in that their displacement was only 7,000 tons level. At time of completion, the 20-cm. guns were mounted in single turrets and the torpedo tubes were stationary. Through conversion of 1937-39, the main guns were mounted in twin turrets and the torpedo tubes in quadruple swivel banks on the upper deck. In the Pacific War, The *Furutaka* Class ships and the *Aoba* Class ships comprised the Sixth Cruiser Division and engaged actively in first line operations until they were sunk in the Solomons area.

Comparable Ships: *Hawkins* (Br.) as originally built, *York* and *Exeter* (Br.) after conversion

(Right): The heavy cruiser *FURUTAKA*, 1930.

CA FURUTAKA.

1) **Displacement.**   ca. 8,000 T. (WS), 9,000 t. (WT)
   Dimensions :   *Length :*   602.16 ft.-183.53 m. (o.a.)
                       Beam :   51.74 ft.-15.77 m. (w.l.)   *Draught :*   18.26 ft.-5.56 m. (mean)
   Armament :   *Guns :*   6–7.9 in., 4–3.1 in. AA.   *Torpedo Tubes :*   12–24 in.   *Planes :* 1
   Machinery :   Kanpon Turbines   *S.H.P. :*   102,000   *Speed :*   34.50 kts.

2) **Displacement.**   9,150 T. (WS), 10,507 t. (WT)
   Dimensions :   *Length :*   595.04 ft.-181.36 m. (w.l.)
                       Beam :   55.53 ft.-16.93 m. (w.l.)   *Draught :*   18.41 ft.-5.61 m. (mean)
   Armament :   *Guns :*   6-8 in., 4-4.7 in. AA.   *Torpedo Tubes :*   8-24 in.
                   Planes :   2   *Catapult :*   1
   Machinery :   Kanpon Turbines   *S.H.P. :*   103,340   *Speed :*   32.95 kts.
   Data :   (*FURUTAKA*)., 1) At completion., 2) After conversion.

KAKO

(Right) :   The heavy cruiser *KAKO*, 1930. The *Furutaka* Class was
conceived at a time when light cruisers of 5,500-ton size (*Kuma*,
Isuzu and *Naka* Classes) were under construction. The techniques
to minimize displacement and at the same time to fit the maximum
armament, realised successfully on the *YUBARI* Class. To achieve
lighter weight, the 20-cm. main guns had to be mounted in single
makeshift turrets. Standard displacement of the ship at completion,
however, was nearly 8,000 tons.

CA KAKO.

AOBA Class

Name	Completed	Converted	Fate
AOBA	20–9–27 Nagasaki	30–10–40	Scrapped after war
KINUGASA	30–9–27 Kawasaki	30–10–40	Lost 14–11–42, Battle of Guadalcanal, U.S. planes

Project: New Reinforcement Programme under Washington Naval Treaty in 1923.

History: Improved from but similar in main particulars to the *Furutaka* Class, the *Aoba* Class ships had from the beginning the main guns mounted in twin turrets and were also equipped with 12-cm. (4.7-in.) anti-aircraft guns. The torpedo tubes, however, were stationary until mounted in quadruple swivel banks on the upper deck through conversion of 1940. The *Aoba* Class were the first Japanese cruisers fitted with aircraft catapults from the outset. Operating with the *Furutaka* Class ships during the war, the *AOBA* survived the war despite damage received in several battles.

Comparable Ships: *York* (Br.) *25 de Mayo* (Arg.)

1) **Displacement:** 8,300 T. (WS)

Dimensions: Length: 602.33 ft.-183.58 m. (w.l.) Beam: 51.94 ft.-15.83 m. (f.l.)
Draught: 18.73 ft.-5.71 m. (mean)

Aramament: Guns: 6-8 . in., 4-4.7 in. AA. Torpedo Tubes: 12-24 in.
Plane: 1 Catap'' : 1

Machinery: Kanpon Turbines S.H.P.: 102,000 Speed: 34.5 kts.

(Right): The heavy cruiser *AOBA* at Yokosuka, 1927.

CA AOBA.

2) **Displacement:** 9,380 T. (WS), 10,822 t. (WT)
Dimensions: *Length:* 594.04 ft.-181.36 m. (w.l.)
Beam: 53.64 ft.-17.60 m. (f.l.) *Draught:* 18.79 ft.-5.66 m. (mean)
Armament: *Guns:* 6-8 in., 4-4.7 in. AA. 8-25 mm. AA., 4-13 mm. AA. *Torpedo Tubes:* 8-24 in.
Planes: 2 *Catapult:* 1
Machinery: Kanpon Turbines *S.H.P.:* 108,456 *Speed:* 33.4 kts.
Data: 1) At completion., 2) After conversion. (AOBA)

CAs KAKO & KINUGASA.

KAKO and KINUGASA

Heavy cruisers *KAKO* (foreground) and *KINUGASA* in 1941 after conversion. Both underwent extensive conversion compared with other heavy cruisers. On catapults are Type 94-2 float reconnaissance biplanes.

The *KINUGASA* in 1927. Speed indicators are on the main mast.

MYOKO Class

Name	Completed	Converted	Fate
MYOKO	31- 7-29 Yokosuka	1) 3/36 2) 30-4-41	Lost 8-7-46, Malacca Strait, Scuttled by British Navy
NACHI	26-11-28 Kure	1) 7/36 2) 3/40	Lost 8-1-44, Manila Bay, U.S. planes
ASHIGARA	20- 8-29 Kawasaki	1) 3/36 2) 6/40	Lost 8-1-45, Banka Strait, British submarine
HAGURO	25- 4-29 Nagasaki	1) 3/36 2) 28-12-39	Lost 16-5-45 Off Penang, British Destroyers

Project: 1923 New Reinforcement Programme under Washington Naval Treaty.

History: Designed by Vice Admiral Y.Hiraga, the *Myoko* Class ships were the first-generation 10,000-ton heavy cruisers to achieve the maximum armament and performance within the limitations of the Washington Naval Treaty. In 1936 the first conversion was made on these ships. The *ASHIGARA*, following conversion, was dispatched in 1936 to England to take part in the international naval review in celebration of the Coronation of King George VI. Through the second conversion the *Myoko* Class ships were modernised and were thrown into the Pacific War on active service. Comprising the Fifth Cruiser Division, all of the *Myoko* Class ships were lost in action.

Comparable Ships: *Pennsacola* (U.S.), *Northampton* (Br.), *Kent* (Br.), *Trento* (It.)

(Right):

The heavy cruiser *MYOKO* in 1932 as the first ship of the Fourth Cruiser Division, flying the colours of the commander.

CA MYOKO.

CA MYOKO.

The *MYOKO* on her official full speed trial run in March 1941 following the second conversion.

(Right): The heavy cruiser *NACHI* at Yokosuka in December 1928. In the right background is seen part of the carrier *HOSHO*. The *NACHI* was the first ship to be completed of the *Myoko* Class. Like the *FURUTAKA*, displacement of the *NACHI* was greater than originally envisaged.

1) **Displacement :**   10,940 T. (WS)   12,374 t. (WT)
    Dimensions :   *Length :*   661.12 ft.-201.50 m. (w.l.)
                          Beam :   56.89 ft.-17.34 m. (f.l.)   *Draught :*   19.36 ft.-5.90 m. (mean)
    Armament :   *Guns :*   10-8 in., 6-4.7 in. AA.   *Torpedo Tubes :*   12-24 in.
                          Planes :   2   *Catapult :*   1
    Machinery :   Kanpon Turbines   S.H.P.:   130,000   *Speed :*   35.5 kts.

CA NACHI.

2) **Displacement :** 13,380 T. (WS), 14,980 t, (WT)
   Dimensions : Length : 661.78 ft.-201.70 m. (w.l.)
                     Beam : 68.02 ft.-20.73 m. (f.l.)   Draught : 20.74 ft.-6.32 m. (mean)
   Armament : Guns : 10-8 in., 8-5 in. AA., 8-25 mm. AA., 4-12.7 mm. AA.   Torpedo Tubes :
                   16-24 in.   Planes : 3   Catapults : 2
   Machinery : Kanpon Turbines   S.H.P.: 130,250   Speed : 33.8 kts.
   Data : 1) At completion. (HAGURO), 2) After conversion (MYOKO).

HAGURO

(Right) : The heavy cruiser *HAGURO* in 1932. The Washington
Naval Treaty started a race, in which the U.S., Britain, France,
Italy, and Japan competed for the construction of the best heavy
cruiser within the limitations of 10,000-tonnage and the 8-in. main
armament. The *Myoko* Class cruiser, the *HAGURO* being the last
to be completed, had two more 8-in. guns and a better speed of
35 kts. compared with the 10,000-ton counterparts of the U.S. and
Britain. (Although this was achieved by ignoring the tonnage limitations)

CA HAGURO.

ASHIGARA

(Below): The heavy cruiser *ASHIGARA* in December 1940 after the second conversion. Note the foremast which is a light tripod mast. In 1942, the *ASHIGARA* took part in the operation against the Dutch East Indies as the flagship of the Third Fleet.

CA ASHIGÁRA.

(Right):

The *ASHIGARA* in 1932. Note differences from the picture on Page 93 in the upper bridge structure, fore and main masts, anti-aircraft armament, the derricks, etc.

CA ASHIGARA.

TAKAO Class

Name	Completed	Converted	Fate
TAKAO	31–5–32 Yokohama	31–8–39	Lost 21-10-46, Malacca Strait, Scuttled by British Navy
ATAGO	30–3–32 Kure	10–39	Lost 23-10-44, Battle for Leyte Gulf, U.S. submarine
MAYA	30–6–32 Kawasaki	3–44	Lost 23-10-44, Battle for Leyte Gulf, U.S. submarine
CHOKAI	30–6–32 Nagasaki		Lost 25-10-44, Battle for Leyte Gulf, U.S. planes

Project: Reinforcement Programme, 1927.

History: Improvement of the *Myoko* Class, the cruisers of the *Takao* Class featured the huge, castle-like bridge structure. The *MAYA* in 1944 came to possess the heaviest anti-aircraft armament among the Japanese heavy cruisers with removal of one 20 cm. main gun turret for the total of 12-12.7-cm. (5 in.) AA. guns and a good number of machine guns. During the war, the *Takao* Class comprised the Fourth Cruiser Division and saw active service until all but the *TAKAO* were sunk in the Battle for Leyte Gulf. The *CHOKAI* will be remembered as the flagship of Admiral Mikawa's Eighth Fleet which scored an overwhelming victory in the Battle of Savo.

Comparable Ships: *Northampton* (U.S.), *Portland* (U.S.), *Dorsetshire* (Br.), *Algérie* (Fr.), *Zara* (It.).

(Right): The heavy cruiser *TAKAO* dressed for the Naval Review of 1923.

CA TAKAO.

CA TAKAO.

ATAGO (Right):

The heavy cruiser *ATAGO* shortly after completion in 1932. While the *TAKAO* had the torpedo tubes on the 'tween deck, the *ATAGO* had four twin tubes on the upper deck, two on each side. Firing rate was one salvo of torpedoes approximately every three minutes. The main guns of the *ATAGO* had a maximum elevation of 70 degrees for anti-aircraft barrage. Thus the *ATAGO* had two anti-aircraft guns less than the *Myoko* Class.

TAKAO (Above):

The heavy cruiser *TAKAO* on her official trial run in 1939 after conversion. The bridge structure was simplified and the main mast was relocated further astern for better efficiency of the radio antennas. Four 5-inch AA. guns were installed just prior to the war.

1)	Displacement :	11,350 T. (WS), 12,986 t. (WT).
	Dimensions :	Length : 661.58 ft.-201.67 m. (w.l.),
		Beam : 59.16 ft.-18.03 m. (f.l.) Draught : 20.05 ft.-6.11 m. (mean)
	Armament :	Guns : 10-8 in., 4-4.7 in. AA. Torpedo Tubes : 8-24 in.
		Planes : 2 Catapults : 2
	Machinery :	Kanpon Turbines S.H.P.: 130,000 Speed : 35.5 kts.
2)	Displacement :	13,160 T. (WS), 14,989 t. (WT)
	Dimensions :	Length : 661.78 ft.-201.70 m. (w.l.),
		Beam : 68.02 ft.-20.73 m. (f.l.) Draught : 20.74 ft.-6.32 m. (mean)
	Armament :	Guns : 10-8 in., 8-8 in. (MAYA-1943) 8-5 in. AA., 12-5 in. AA. (MAYA-1943)
		60-25 mm. AA. (TAKAO, ATAGO), 66-25 mm. AA. (MAYA) after wartime re-
		equipment. No additional AA. guns fitted on the CHOKAI.
		Torpedo Tubes : 16-24 in. Planes : 3 Catapults : 2
	Machinery :	Kanpon Turbines S.H.P.: 133,100 Speed : 34.25 kts

CHOKAI (2)

(Right): The heavy cruiser CHOKAI at Ariake Bay, Kyushu Island on
30th September 1938. Her foremast is modernised.

CA CHOKAI.

CA CHOKAI.

The heavy cruiser *CHOKAI* as seen from a British ship at Amoy in June 1940. Under the derrick are Type 94 and Type 95 reconaissance float planes. The Type 94 was used mainly for reconaissance while the Type 95 single-float was used for spotting. In a few years these floatplanes were replaced by Type 0 three-seat reconaissance monoplane and Type 0 single-float spotter biplane.

CA MAYA.

The heavy cruiser *MAYA* in 1932. No conversion was made on *MAYA* or *CHOKAI* before the war. In November 1943, the *MAYA* was damaged by air raids at Rabaul and along with repair works extensive conversion was effected. The C turret was removed for four 5-in. AA. guns and a good number of machine guns were added. The bridge of the ships of this class was too large since it accomodated facilities for use of the ship as a war-time emergency flagship of a fleet.

The design and operational concept was criticised and after the *Mogami* Class the size of the bridge was decreased.

MOGAMI Class

Name	Completed	Converted		Fate
MOGAMI	28-7-35 Kure	1)	**12-39**	Lost 25-10-44, Battle for Leyte Gulf, U.S.
		2) 30- 4-43		planes
MIKUMA	29-8-35 Nagasaki	30-12-39		Lost 6-6-42, Battle for Midway, U.S. planes
SUZUYA	31-10-37 Yokosuka	30-12-39		Lost 25-10-44, Battle for Leyte Gulf, U.S. planes
KUMANO	31-10-37 Kawasaki	30-12-39		Lost 25-11-44, at Colon Bay, U.S. planes

Project: First Reinforcement Programme under London Naval Treaty, 1931.

History: Due to restrictions brought about by the London Naval Treaty, the *Mogami* Class was conceived as large light cruisers carrying fifteen 15.5-cm. (6.1-in.) guns in five triple turrets, which would be a good much for the 8-in. guns of the 10,000-ton heavy cruisers. The *Mogami* Class, first Japanese warships to have triple turrets, was named after famous rivers in Japan, being light cruiser at birth. In 1939, however, all four ships of the *Mogami* Class were converted to carry ten 20-cm. main guns in lieu of 15.5-cm. guns to become heavy cruisers. The *Mogami* Class comprised the Seventh Cruiser Division and engaged in most major battles.

The *MIKUMA* put up a heroic battle to save the damaged *MOGAMI* in the Battle of Midway in 1942 to become the first Japanese heavy cruiser to be lost in the Pacific War. The *MOGAMI*, through repair and reconstruction, became a carrier-cruiser, carrying 11 float reconnaissance planes on the flight deck which replaced the Nos. 4 and 5 turrets.

(Right): The heavy cruiser *MOGAMI* at 36-kt. full speed in 1935.

CA MOGAMI.

Comparable Ships : As light cruiser, *Brooklyn* (U.S.), *Southampton* (Br.) As heavy cruiser, *New Orleans* (U.S.), *Algérie* (Fr.), *Admiral Hipper* (Gr.)

1) **Displacement :** 11,200 T. (WS)
   Dimensions :
   Length :   649.83 ft.-198.06 m. (w.l.)
   Beam :   63.00 ft.-19.20 m. (f.l.)   Draught :   19.36 ft.-5.90 m. (mean)
   Armament : Guns :   15-6.1 in. 8-5 in. AA.   Torpedo Tubes :   12-24 in.
   Planes :   3   Catapults :   2
   Machinery : Kanpon Turbines   S.H.P.: 152,000   Speed : 35.9 kts.

2) **Displacement :** 12,400 T. (WS), 13,887 t. (WT)
   Dimensions :
   Length :   649.83 ft.-198.06 m. (w.l.)
   Beam :   66.28 ft.-20.20 m. (f.l.)   Draught :   19.36 ft.-5.90 m. (mean)
   Armament : Guns :   10-8 in. 8-5 in. AA. 8-25 mm. AA. 4-12.7 mm. AA.   Torpedo Tubes :   12-24 in.
   Planes :   3   Catapults :   2
   Machinery : Kanpon Turbines   S.H.P.: 152,000   Speed : 34.7 kts.
   Data : 1) As light cruiser., 2) After conversion to heavy cruiser (MOGAMI)

MIKUMA

(Right) : The heavy cruiser *MIKUMA* at Hakodate in September 1935. Note the arrangement of the fore turrets which differs from that of the *Takao* Class, which gives a wider field of fire to the No.3 turret. On each side of the ship are two triple torpedo tube banks. Anti-aircraft armament of this class was heavier than that of 10,000-ton class cruisers, having eight 12.7-cm. (5 in.) guns. The two white stripes around the funnel denotes the second ship of the Seventh Cruiser Division. The ship is seen carrying a Type 90 Model 3 float reconnaissance biplane.

CA MIKUMA.

SUZUYA

The heavy cruiser *SUZUYA* at war exercises in the Pacific south of the Honshu Island in August 1938.

As the white stripes denote, she was the ships of the Seventh Cruiser Division. On the catapults may be seen Type 94 and Type 95 float-planes. The *SUZUYA* was improved in the cause of her construction, overcoming various shortcomings found after completion of the *MOGAMI*. Equipped with 20-cm. (8-in.) guns in 1940, the *SUZUYA* become the most powerful heavy cruiser of the Imperial Japanese Navy.

CA SUZUYA.

KUMANO

The heavy cruiser *KUMANO* was a development of the *Mogami* Class, together with her sister ship *SUZUYA*. The only modification after completion was the replacememement of 6.1-in. main guns with 8-in. guns. Quite a few gunnery experts, however, were against this replacement since salvoes from fifteen 6.1-in. guns were as effective as those from ten 8-in. guns.

CA KUMANO.

TONE Class

Name	Completed	Fate
TONE	20-11-38 Nagasaki	Scrapped after war
CHIKUMA	20-5-39 Nagasaki	Lost 25-10-44, Battle for Leyte Gulf, U.S.

Project: Second Reinforcement Programme, 1934.

History: Improvement of *Mogami* Class, the *Tone* Class was originally designed as light cruisers with 15.5-cm. (6.1-in) guns. During construction, however, the naval treaty expired and the *TONE* and *CHIKUMA* finally emerged as heavy cruisers with eight 20-cm. (8-in.) main guns. As in *DUNKERQUE* (Fr.) and *NELSON* (Br.), the main armament was concentrated on the fore deck.

On the spacious aft deck the *Tone* Class carried five reconnaissance floatplanes. During the Pacific War, the *TONE* and *CHIKUMA* comprised the Eighth Cruiser Division and operated with carrier task forces.

Comparable Ships: *Witchita* (U.S.), *Admiral Hipper* (Gr.)

Displacement:	11,900 T. (WS), 14,070 t. (WT)
Dimensions:	*Length:* 661.45 ft.-201.60 m. (o.a.), 649.64 ft.-198.00 m. (w.l.)
	Beam: 60.68 ft.-18.50 m. (f.l.) *Draught:* 20.44 ft.-6.23 m. (mean)
Armament:	*Guns:* 8-8 in. 8-5 in. AA. 8-25 mm. AA. 4-12.7 mm.
	Torpedo Tubes: 12-24 in. *Planes:* 6 *Catapults:* 2
Machinery:	Kanpon Turbines *S.H.P.:* 152,200 *Speed:* 35.0 kts.

(Right): The heavy cruiser *TONE* as seen from the *CHIKUMA* during the naval manoeuvres of 1940.

CA TONE. *113*

LIGHT CRUISERS

TENRYU Class

Name	Completed	Fate
TENRYU	20-11-19 Yokosuka	Lost 18-12-42, in Bismarck Sea, U.S. submarine
TATSUTA	31-3-19 Sasebo	Lost 13-3-44, off Hachijojima, U.S. submarine

Project: New Shipbuilding Programme of 1916.

History: The *Tenryu* Class were the first modern light cruisers of the Imperial Japanese Navy, built to cope with the *Aurora* Class of Britain. They were also the first Japanese warships to carry torpedo tubes in triple mounts. Until completion of the 5,500-ton light cruisers, they were used as the flagships of destroyer squadrons.

These obsolete cruisers formed the 18th Squadron during the Pacific War. The *TENRYU* took part in the Battle of Savo.

Comparable Ships: *C* Class (Br.)

Displacement: 3,230 T. (WS), 3,948 t. (WN)

Dimensions: Length: 457.90 ft.-139.56 m. (w.l.) Beam: 40.49 ft.-12.34 m. (f.l.) Draught: 12.99 ft.-3.96 m. (mean)

Armament: Guns: 4-5.5 in. Torpedo Tubes: 6-21 in.

Machinery: Curtis Turbines S.H.P.: 51,000 Speed: 33.0 kts.

(Right): The light cruiser *TENRYU* at Yokohama on 12th April 1922.

CL TENRYU.

CL TATSUTA.

TATSUTA

(Above): The light cruiser *TATSUTA* in 1931, with the fore-mast converted to the tripod mast.

(Right): The light cruiser *TATSUTA* as the flagship of the First Destroyer Squadron in 1927.

CL TATSUTA.

KUMA Class

Name	Completed	Converted	Fate
KUMA	31-8-20 Sasebo	1934	Lost 11-1-44, off Penang, British submarine
TAMA	29-1-21 Nagasaki	1) 1934 2) 1944	Lost 25-10-44, Battle for Leyte Gulf, U.S. submarine
KITAKAMI	15-4-21 Sasebo	1) 12-41 2) 1-45	Scrapped after war
OOI	3-10-21 Kawasaki	9-41	Lost 19-7-44, in South China Sea, U.S. submarine
KiSO	4-5-21 Nagasaki		Lost 13-11-44, off Manila, U.S. Planes

Project : 8-4 Fleet Project of 1917.
History : The *Kuma* Class were the first of the 5,500-ton series of light cruisers, developed from the *Tenryu* Class. Remained in active service until all but the *KITAKAMI* were sunk in action. The *OOI* and *KITAKAMI* were converted into mother ships for the Kaiten human torpedoes in 1945. The *TAMA* and *KISO* belonged to the Fifth Fleet which operated for the defence of the Northern Pacific.

Comparable Ships : *D* Class (Br.)
Displacement : 5,100 T. (WS), 5,500 T. (WN)
Dimensions : Length : 520.12 ft.-158.53 m (w.l.) Beam : 46.49 ft.-14.17 m. (f.l.)
Draught : 15.75 ft.-4.80 m. (mean)
Armament : Guns : 7-5.5 in. Torpedo Tubes : 8-21 in. Plane : 1 Catapult : 1
Machinery : Gihon Turbines S.H.P.: 90,000 Speed : 36.0 kts

(Right) : The light cruiser *KUMA* at Tateyama in March 1924.

CL KUMA.

After conversion as torpedo ship (*KITAKAMI*)

Displacement :	5,870 T. (WS)
Aramament :	Guns : 4-5.5 in. Torpedo Tubes : 40-24 in.
Machinery :	Gihon Turbines S.H.P. : 90,000 Speed : 31.4 kts.

(Right) : The light cruiser *TAMA* entering Yokosuka harbour in the summer of 1934. The bridge is sheltered by canvas.

(Below) :
The light cruiser *KUMA* in June 1935 was the flagship of the Fifth Fleet. On the catapult is a Type 90 Model 2-2 floatplane.

CL KUMA.

CL TAMA.

KITAKAMI

The light cruiser *KITAKAMI* in late 1920s. During modification in 1934 the No. 1 funnel of the *KITAKAMI* was a little extended, which distinguished it from her sister ships.

CL KITAKAMI.

NAGARA Class

Name	Completed	Converted	Fate
NAGARA	21-4-22 Sasebo	1934	Lost 7-8-44, south of Kyushu, U.S. submarine
ISUZU	15-8-23 Uraga	1) 1934 2) 1944	Lost 7-4-45, off Sunbawa, U.S. submarine
NATORI	15-9-22 Nagasaki	1934	Lost 18-8-44, off Samar. U.S. submarine
YURA	20-3-23 Sasebo	1934	Lost 25-10-42, off Santa Isabel, U.S. planes
KINU	10-11-22 Kawasaki	1934	Lost 26-10-44, off Masbate, U.S. submarine
ABUKUMA	26-5-25 Uraga	1934	Lost 25-10-44, Battle for Leyte Gulf, U.S. planes

Project: 8-4 Fleet - 8-8 Fleet Programme (1917-20)

History: Improvement of the *Kuma* Class, the *Nagara* Class was similar in silhouette but differed greatly in that ships of the *Nagara* Class were the first to be equipped with 61-cm. torpedo tubes. The *Nagara* Class cruisers were actually used in the war as flagships of cruiser, destroyer and submarine squadrons. Through renovation in 1934, the tripod main-mast, the derrick and the catapult were installed. The *ISUZU* was converted in 1944 as an anti-aircraft cruiser.

Comparable Ships: *D* and *C* Classes (Br.), *Omaha* (U.S.)

(Right): The light cruiser *NATORI* in late 1920s.

CL NATORI

Displacement :	5,170 T. (WS), 5,570 t. (WN)			
Dimensions :	Length : 520.12 ft.-158.53 m. (w.l.)		Beam : 46.49 ft.-14.17 m. (f.l.)	
	Draught : 15.75 ft.-4.80 m. (mean)			
Armament :	Guns : 7-5.5 in.	Torpedo Tubes : 8-24 in.	Plane : 1	Catapult : 1
Machinery :	Gihon Turbines (Curtis Turbines-*KINU* only)		S.H.P. : 90,000	Speed : 36.0 kts.

ABUKUMA (Right): The light cruiser *ABUKUMA* in 1930. The shape of the *ABUKUMA* bow was changed as seen in this photo through repairs of the damage received during the large-scale naval exercises of 1930. All other three-stack light cruisers had racked bows.

YURA (Below): The light cruiser *YURA* in 1937. On the catapult is a Type 90 Model 2 floatplane. Note the tripod mainmast which supports the derrick.

CL YURA.

CL ABUKUMA

127

SENDAI Class

Name	Completed	Conversions	Fate
SENDAI	29-4-24	1) 1937	Lost 1-11-43, Battle of
	Nagasaki	2) 1941	Bougainville, U.S. ships
JINTSU	31-7-25	1) 1934	Lost 13-7-43, Night Battle of
	Kawasaki	2) 1941	Koronbangara, U.S. ships
NAKA	30-11-25	1) 1934	Lost 17-2-44, at Truk,
	Yokohama	2) 1941	U.S. planes

Project : 8-8 Fleet Programme, 1920.

History : The last of the 5,500-ton light cruiser series, the *Sendai* Class ships were all four-stackers. In 1934, the triple mainmast, the derrick and catapult were installed. Prior to the Pacific War, they were again modernised, including fitting of quadruple torpedo tube mounts.

Comparable Ships : *D* and *C* Classes (Br.), *Omaha* (U.S.), *Emden* (Gr.), *Java* (Ned.)

Displacement : 5,195 T. (WS), 5,595 t. (WN)

Dimensions : *Length :* 520.12 ft.-158.53 m. (W.l.) *Beam :* 46.49 ft.-14.17 m. (f.l.),
Draught : 16.11 ft.-4.91 m. (mean)

Armament : *Guns :* 7-5.5 in. *Torpedo Tubes :* 8-24 in. *Plane :* 1
Catapult : 1

Machinery : Gihon Turbines (Curtis Turbines-*JINTSU* only) *S.H.P. :* 90,000
Speed : 35.25 kts.

(Right) : The light cruiser *JINTSU* in the autumn of 1930. Her original cutter bow was replaced with a double-curvature bow after she lost her bow in a night collision with the destroyer *WARABI* in the Japan Sea in 1927.

CL JINTSU.

SENDAI (Below):

The light cruiser *SENDAI* in August 1937. Note the raked bow of the *SENDAI* which is similar to that of the *Kuma* Class ships. The *SENDAI*'s bow was not changed, while other four-stackers were later fitted with bows of different shape.

NAKA (Right):

The light cruiser *NAKA*, the last to be completed of the *Sendai* Class, had the bow as seen in this picture from the beginning.

(Below) ·

CL SENDAI.

CL NAKA.

YUBARI Class

Name	Completed	Converted	Fate
YUBARI	31-7-23	1934	Lost 27-4-44, off Palau
	Sasebo		U.S. submarine

Project: 8-4 Fleet Programme, 1917.

History: Designed by Vice Admiral Y.Hiraga, the *YUBARI* is world famous for having the armament of a *5,500-ton* Class cruiser with her 2,900-ton displacement. All armament structure was built on the keel-line. The experience in successfully designing the *YU-BARI* contributed greatly to the birth of the *Furutaka* and the subsequent series of heavy cruisers. The anti-aircraft armament and torpedo tubes were augmented in 1934.

Comparable Ships: *Tromp* (Ned.), *Guépard*-as destroyer-(Fr.)

Displacement: 2.890 T. (WS), 3,141 t. (WN)

Dimensions: *Length:* 450.02 ft.-137.16 m. (w.l.)   *Beam:* 39.50 ft.-12.04 m. (max.)
Draught: 11.75 ft.-3.58 m. (mean) (f.l.)

Armament: Guns: 6-5.5 in. 1-3.1 in. AA., (4-5.5 in., 2-5 in. AA., 12-25 mm. AA., 8-13 mm. AA. -1943) Torpedo Tubes: 4-24 in.

Machinery: Gihon Turbines   S.H.P.: 57,900   Speed: 35.5 kts.

(Right): The light cruiser *YUBARI* with lengthened funnel top.
Note positioning of the twin-gun turret at higher level than
that of the single-gun turret to achieve better firing accuracy.

CL YUBARI.

AGANO Class

Name	Completed		Fate
AGANO	31–10–41	Sasebo	Lost 17–2–44, Off Truk, U.S. submarine
NOSHIRO	30– 6–43	Sasebo	Lost 26–10–44, South of Mindro, U.S. planes
YAHAGI	29–12–43	Yokosuka	Lost 7–4–45, Battle of Bonomisaki, U.S. planes
SAKAWA	30–11–44	Kure	Lost 2–7–46, Bikini Atoll, U.S. A-bomb test

Project : Fourth Reinforcement Programme.

History : The light cruiser force of the Imperial Japanese Navy at the outbreak of the Pacific War was far inferior to the heavy cruiser force both quantitatively and qualitatively since new ships of the *Mogami* and *Tone* Classes had been converted into heavy cruisers and only ageing *5,500-ton* Class vessels remained for operational service.

The *Agano* Class ships were excellent light cruisers which could reach the high speed of 35 kts. comparable to modern destroyers. These cruisers were equipped with six 15-cm. (5.9-in.) main guns, eight 61-cm. (24-in.) torpedo tubes, a modern communication system, and increased AA. armament. When the *Agano* Class ships were commissioned in 1943, however, there remained only a few destroyers with which they could from destroyers squadrons. With the air power playing the lead in sea battles, there also was little need for destroyer squadrons. Which might have played havoc in the armada-vs.-armada battle in the Pacific conceived by the Japanese and American long before Pearl Harbour.

Comparable Ships : *Köln* (Gr.), *Arethusa* (Br.)

(Right): The light cruiser *NOSHIRO* on official full power trial run in July 1943.

CL NOSHIRO

Displccement : 6,652 T. (WS), 7,710 t. (WT)

Dimensions . *Length :* 594.16 ft.–172.00 m. (w.l.) *Beam :* 49.86 ft.–15.20 m. (hull) *Draught :* 18.97 ft.– 5.63 m. (mean)

Armament : *Guns :* 6–5.9 in., 4–3.1 in. AA., 6–25 mm. AA. *Torpedo Tubes :* 8–24 in. *Planes :* **2** *Catapult :* 1

Machinery : Kanpon Turbines *S.H.P. :* 100,000 *Speed :* 35.0 kts.

YAHAGI (Right)

The light cruiser *YAHAGI* at Lingga, off Sumatra, in October 1944, prior to the Battle for the Leyte Gulf. She carried two Type 0 three-seat twin-float reconnaissance monoplanes. In the right background is the light cruiser *NOSHIRO*.

CL YAHAGI

OYODO Class

Name	Completed	Conversion	Fate
OYODO	28-2-43 Kure	—44	Scrapped after war

Project : Fourth Reinforcement Programme.

History : The *Oyodo* Class was projected as flagships for submarine flotillas and comprised the *OYODO* and the *NIYODO*.

Construction of the *NIYODO* however was cancelled immediately before the outbreak of the Pacific War, the *OYODO* being the sole ship of this class ever built.

A unique feature of the *OYODO* as a light cruiser lay in the fact that it had no torpedo tubes but was to carry six high-speed reconnaissance floatplanes. *OYODO* however had good communication equipment and the Naval High Command decided to use her as the flagship on the Combined Fleet. Early 1944, the *OYODO* conversion was completed at Yokosuka, the large hangar being modified into operations and living quarters and the 45-m. catapult replaced with a 25-m. standard catapult.

In October 1944, the *OYODO* was with the Third Fleet (Adm. J. Ozawa) in the Battle for Leyte Gulf and with its powerful radio equipment transmitted the success in the decoy tactics against the Halsey Force to Adm. Kurita's strike force, after Adm. Ozawa had removed

Comparable Ships : *Cleveland* (U.S.), *Southampton* (Br.), *Kirov* (Sov.)

Displacement : 8,164 T.(WS), 9,980 t.(WT)

Dimensions : Length : 619.92 ft.–189.00 m.(w.l.)   Beam : 54.40 ft.–16.60 m.(hull)   Draught : 19.52 ft.–5.95 m.(mean)

Armament : Guns : 6–6.1 in., 8–3.9 in. AA., 12–25 mm. AA.   Planes : 6   Catapult : 1

Machinery : Kanpon Turbines   S.H.P.: 110,000   Speed : 35.0 kts.

The light cruiser *OYODO*, as just commissioned.

CL OYODO

TRAINING CRUISERS

KATORI Class

Name	Completed	Converted	Fate
KATORI	20-4-40 Yokohama		Lost 17-2-44, at Truk, U.S. ships and planes
KASHIMA	31-5-40 Yokohama	1944	Scrapped after war
KASHII	15-7-41 Yokohama	1944	Lost 12-1-45, in South China Sea, U. S. planes
KASHIWARA	Construction started in August 1941 but was dismantled due to the outbreak of the Pacific War.		

Project: Third Reinforcement Programme of 1937 (*KATORI* and *KASHIMA*). Fourth Reinforcement Programme of 1939 (*KASHII*). Supplementary Programme of 1940 (*KASHIWARA*).

History: Named after the old shrines, the *Katori* Class ships were designed and built exclusively for training naval cadets in ocean cruising. The *KATORI* and *KASHIMA* each only could make one ocean cruise because of the war. The *Katori* Class ships were utilized as flagships of the 6th Fleet (*KATORI*), 4th Fleet (*KASHIMA*), and Southern Detachment Fleet (*KASHII*). Later the *KASHIMA* and *KASHII* were converted for anti-submarine duties.

Comparable ships: *Jeanne d'Arc* (Fr.)

Displacement: 5,890 T. (WS), 6,300 t. (WT)
Dimensions: Length: 426.53 ft.-130.00 m. (w.l.) Beam: 52.33 ft.-15.95 m. (f.l.)
Draught: 18.87 ft.-5.75 m. (mean)

Armament: Guns: 4-5.5 in., 2-5 in. AA., 4-25 mm. AA.   Torpedo Tubes: 4-21 in.
Plane: 1   Catapult: 1
Turbines and Diesels   Total H.P.: 8,000   Speed: 18.0 kts.

Training CL KATORI.

KATORI   The training cruiser *KATORI* shortly after completion. Behind the funnel is seen the catapult, covered with a canvas sheet.

Battleships on anchor in Sukumo Bay, Shikoku Island, May 1937.
From left to right, the *HYUGA*, the *NAGATO*, and the *MUTSU* of the First Battleship Division; the *HARUNA* and the *KIRISHIMA* of the Third Battleship Division.

Heavy Cruisers on anchor in Beppu Bay, Kyushu Island, in the autumn of 1933. From foreground, the *CHOKAI*, the *MAYA*, the *TAKAO*, the *ATAGO*, the *AOBA*, the *KINUGASA*, and the *KAKO*. In left background are 5,500-ton light cruisers.

Destroyers leaving Sukumo Bay in May 1937. Battleships in the background are, from left, the *HARUNA*, the *HYUGA*, the *MUTSU*, and the *NAGATO*.
The Heavy cruiser *TAKAO* and light cruisers of the *Sendai* Class are also seen in the picture.

Photo Credits: A number of photographs in this book have been made available through 'Sekai-no-Kansen' 〈Ships of the World〉 magazine; Nihon Eiga Shinsha, Messrs. Akira Furukawa, Motoyoshi Hori, Ryozo Honda and Yoshikatsu Tomioka.

SILHOUETTES

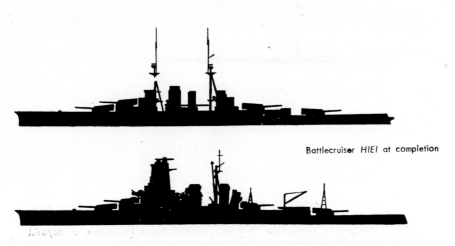

Battlecruiser *HIEI* at completion

Battleship *KONGO* after second conversion.

Battleship *FUSO* at completion

Battleship *FUSO* after conversion.

Battleship *YAMASHIRO* after conversion

147

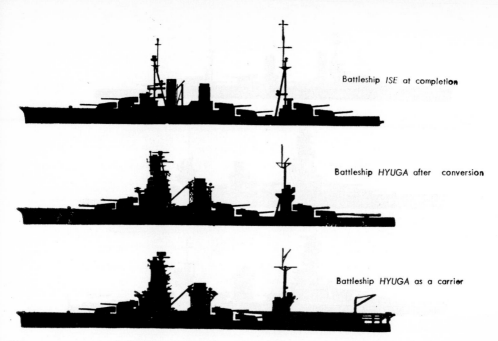

Battleship *ISE* at completion

Battleship *HYUGA* after conversion

Battleship *HYUGA* as a carrier